The Paul Story

Musings for Meditation and Application

John Sawyer

Parson's Porch Books
www.parsonsporchbooks.com

The Paul Story: Musings for Meditation and Application
ISBN: Softcover 978-1-949888-51-5
Copyright © 2019 by John Sawyer

All rights reserved. No part of this book may be reproduced or transmitted in any form or by any means, electronic or mechanical, including photocopying, recording, or by any information storage and retrieval system, without permission in writing from the publisher.

The Paul Story

Contents

Introduction 9

Saul the Pharisee 11

The Conversion Story 14

    Acts 7:54-60; 8:1-3; 9:1-19; 22:3-16; 26:1-23;Galatians 1:13; Philippians 3:6

Post Conversion Years 17

    Acts 9:19-30; 2 Corinthians 11:32-33; Galatians 1:13-23

Paul And The Antioch Church 19

    Acts 11:19-30; 13:1-3; 12:25

Paul's First Missionary Journey 21

    Acts 13:2-52; 14:1-28

Paul and Barnabas Separated 25

    Acts 15:36-40

Paul and Silas and Letter of Galatians 28

    Acts 15:36-41 & Galatians

Paul and Silas in Derbe, Lystra 31

    Acts 15:40-41; 16:1-5

Paul's Call to Europe 34

    Acts 16:6-10

Paul and Companions in Philippi: Lydia, the First Convert in Europe 37

    Acts 16:11-15

Paul and Companions in Philippi; The Slave Girl 40

    Acts 16:16-18

Paul and Companions in Philippi: The Philippian Jailer .. 43

    Acts 16:19-40

Paul And Silas In Thessalonica 46
    Acts 17:1-15
Paul Alone in Athens 49
    Acts 17:16-34
Paul in Corinth and Return to Antioch 52
    Acts 18:1-22
Paul at Ephesus 59
    Acts 18:23-28; 19:1-20)
Paul and the Uproar in Ephesus 62
    Acts 19:21-41
Paul in Greece and Troas 65
    Acts 20:1-12
Paul Sailed to Caesarea 69
    Acts 21:1-14
Paul Met With the Ephesian Elders at Miletus 72
    Acts 20:13-38
Paul Sailed to Caesarea 75
    Acts 21:1-14
Paul Met With the Jerusalem Church 78
    Acts 21:15-26
Paul Arrested in Jerusalem 81
    Acts 21:27-40; 22:1-29
Paul Before Felix 84
    Acts 24:1-27
Paul Before the Sanhedrin and Escorted to Caesarea 87
    Acts 22:30 23:1-35

Paul Before Festus and Agrippa 90
    Acts 25:1-27; 26:1-32
Paul's Voyage and Shipwreck 93
    Acts 27:1-44
Paul on Malta and on to Rome 96
    Acts 28:1-10; Acts 28: 11-31 99

Introduction

The Bible tells two stories of the Apostle Paul. One story is told in the Acts of the Apostles by Luke, believed by many to be the author. In fact, the greater part of Acts is about Paul. That being so, you may wonder why the book isn't called Acts of Paul and a Few Other Apostles.

The second story of Paul is gathered from the biographical material in the thirteen letters in the New Testament attributed to him in their salutations. Most of the letters are written to churches, but a few to individuals. These letters are from Romans through Philemon. The order has nothing to do with the sequence in which they were written. In your study, you may discover some discrepancies in the two stories. Probably, most Bible scholars believe that Paul wrote only 8 of the letters attributed to him. Those letters are Romans, I & II Corinthians, Galatians, Philippians, Colossians, I Thessalonians and Philemon. Some scholars question if Paul would have used some of the words or Greek moral codes used in the disputed letters. There are also doubts if church development and leader titles, in questioned letters, were in use in Paul's time. For this study all thirteen will be referenced as belonging to Paul. Bible quotes are from the new Revised Standard Version and The New International Version. There are some questions you may raise as you read the stories about Paul. It seems natural to compare what Paul did and said to what you know about Jesus from the Gospel stories. The churches and Christians you know may be more Pauline than Christian.

The beliefs of many persons and churches are derived from Paul's writing. Many church disputes and "splits" are over beliefs. Jesus seemed to be more concerned that those of the Way follow him in attitude, word and acts. There seemed to be a lot less of what you have to believe to be Christian in the Gospels than in Paul's writing. Most of the "formulas" for becoming a Christian are put together with verses from Paul's writing. Though Paul did write several "sin" lists, he seemed to major on what one had to accept as his gospel.

By the way, it is from those lists that people pick and choose the sins they consider the most deadly and evil. The ones chosen are usually the ones that the person thinks he does not commit.

Keep in mind as you read Paul's writing that you are hearing what Paul wrote, but may not have a full grasp of the problem to which he is speaking. It is like hearing one side of a telephone conversation. It is reading letters that are responses to letters received; problems heard about; and personal concerns and truth that Paul desires to convey to the readers. The purpose of this study is to help the reader get a better grasp of Paul's story and through meditation and questioning discover ways to be a better follower of Jesus. The idea is to study Paul in the light of the life and teachings of Jesus. "The Jesus Story: Musings for Meditation and Application" might give additional help. Each chapter in this book will also close with an Application to Life challenge. This book is designed for individual and group study.

Saul the Pharisee

To begin our study of the Apostle Paul we need to know what we can about his life before becoming a "Christian." I put the word in quotation marks because in Paul's time the followers of Jesus seemed to be known as those of the "Way." Some have questioned that Jesus or Paul intended to start a new religion. That is, were those of the "Way" a sect of Judaism?

Suppose we make an attempt to write a resume' for Paul. How do you think it would look?

The Apostle Paul

Name: Saul (Hebrew), Paul (Greek)

Home Town: Tarsus "I am a Jew born in Tarsus in Cilicia" Acts 22:3

Parents: One must have had Roman Citizenship. Paul said. "I was born a (Roman) citizen" Acts 22:28b. Read the discussion Paul had with the Roman centurion about Roman Citizenship in Acts 22:25-29.

Married?? Was marriage a requirement to be a Pharisee? He did have a sister and nephew who saved Paul from an ambush, Acts 23:16

Education: Leather worker or tent maker training. Schooled in Jewish belief, history and law at synagogue in early life? Educated in Jewish belief, history and law by Gamaliel.

"...but brought up in this city (Jerusalem?) at the feet of Gamaliel" Acts 22:3.

Early Religious Calling: Pharisee of the highest order."...I have belonged to the strictest sect of our religion and lived as a Pharisee" Acts 26:5. "...circumcised on the eighth day, a member of the people of Israel, of the tribe of Benjamin, a Hebrew born of Hebrews; as to the law, a Pharisee; as to zeal, a persecutor of the church; as to righteousness under the law, blameless" Philippians 3:5-6.

Accomplishments: Member of Jewish Council (Sanhedrin? the Jewish highest court). Persecutor of those of the Jesus "Way." "I not only locked up many of saints in prison, but I also cast my vote against them when they were being condemned to death.... I was so furiously enraged at them, I pursued them even to foreign cities" Acts 26:9-11.

Later Religious Calling: Apostle of Jesus Christ par excellent. That is the theme of this study.

Application to Life

Write your own story from earliest memories to the time you became a follower of Jesus.

Watch how your early learning experiences affected how you thought about everything.

Find the words to "You Have to be Taught to Hate" from the old musical South Pacific. How true are these words to you? What about Saul? If you are in a study group, spend time discussing the song. Do we as a society and church give too little emphasis to early childhood education?

The Conversion Story
Acts 7:54-60; 8:1-3; 9:1-19; 22:3-16; 26:1-23; Galatians 1:13; Philippians 3:6

We first meet Saul (Hebrew), later called Paul (his Roman name), at the execution of a Jesus follower named Stephen. He was being stoned to death and Saul, a young man, was guarding the coats of those who were casting the deadly stones. Saul approved the stoning of Stephen.

In fact, Saul had a vicious desire to ravage the church. He apparently was going door to door to find followers of Jesus and taking them, men and women to prison.

Saul's story picks up with chapter 9. His search and arrest activity have moved beyond Jerusalem to Damascus in Syria, over one hundred miles away. It was on this journey as he and his posse came near Damascus a blinding light knocked Saul to the ground and blinded him. He heard a voice asking why he was persecuting the one speaking. Saul asked for his identity and the response was Jesus. Saul was told that it was difficult to kick against the pricks. This metaphor is that of an oxen driver who prods the animal in the right direction.

Do you think this refers to a gnawing at Saul's conscience, his stubbornness toward the truth about Jesus? Do you think the message of Stephen and observance of his death was getting to Saul? The voice tells Saul that he is to be a messenger to the Gentiles. This blinding experience was so real to Saul that he will make the claim that he has seen the risen Christ. He was sure that it was the voice of Jesus that he heard.

In Damascus a very brave follower of Jesus, Ananias, was told in a vision that he is to go to see Saul. He reminded the Lord of Saul's character, but went to find Saul, touched him and Saul was healed of his blindness, filled with Holy Spirit, baptized and began preaching that Jesus is the Son of God. Saul never grew tired of telling his story. Luke has him tell or refer to his call several times in Acts. It is at least referenced in at least four of his letters as you will note in the scripture for this and other studies.

Saul became as radical for Christ as he was in opposition to him. He very soon learned, even while still in Damascus, that suffering is part of the call. He immediately began to preach, but soon ran into opposition himself. He went to Arabia? Why? That is part of the next study.

Application to Life

Do you think Saul thought he was doing God's will when he persecuted Jesus' followers?

Do you think the light that blinded Saul was lightening? Or was it something else?

What part did Saul's conscience play in his conversion experience?

Share your "call" to be a person of the Way.

Do you know someone who had a radical change in becoming a follower of Jesus?

Do you think God uses the circumstances of life to speak to us?

Have you had the opportunity to stand in support of one who has had a radical change?

Post Conversion Years
Acts 9:19-30; 2 Corinthians 11:32-33; Galatians 1:13-23

The scripture lesson for this study is rather brief but covers a number of years in the life of the new convert, Saul. It seems his immediate change and preaching that Jesus is the son of God and the expected Jewish Messiah (Hebrew), Christ (Greek) got him in trouble with his former anti Jesus friends. So, Saul goes to Arabia. Where in Arabia did he go? Why may have several answers. Some think he fled for safety. Some would say it was a mission trip to preach the good news. Others would argue that he was seeking retreat for study, meditation, prayer. Does the last answer remind you of Jesus retreat to the wilderness immediately after his baptism? See Matthew 4:1-11.

Saul returned to Damascus. Brave of him, don't you think? He seems to have spent three years there. There was a plot to kill him, so his friends helped him escape and he finally went back to Jerusalem. Saul did not go to the leaders of the church to seek their approval. In fact, the church was afraid of him. Barnabas came to his rescue and stood up for him as Ananias had done in Damascus. Barnabas will reappear soon in the Saul story. He was a great guy. His birth name was Joseph, but the disciples gave him the name Barnabas, which means son of encouragement. Saul did meet with some the church leaders, James, the brother of Jesus, who seems to be the number one leader in the church at Jerusalem at that time. He also met with Simon Peter, a fisherman, who became one of Jesus' twelve disciples. Several events in the life of Peter are recorded in the first ten chapters of Acts. Trouble followed Saul. Threatened in Jerusalem, the disciples escorted him to the coast city of Caesarea and from there he went home to Tarsus. But everywhere he went he continued to preach that Jesus is Lord.

Application to Life

Discuss why Paul may have fled to Arabia? What do you think he did while there? Make a list of the possibilities: restudy of Scripture (Old Testament); prayer for direction; preach. What else?

Discuss the values of private and group retreats. What about a daily retreat? Is that what daily quiet time, meditation and journaling are about? Saul seemed to discount the value of talking with church leaders. What do you think? Does reading or discussing the ideas of others not help to determine your own ideas and beliefs?

Paul and the Antioch Church
Acts 11:19-30; 13:1-3; 12:25

In the previous study we left Paul in his home city, Tarsus. "He (Saul) spoke and argued with the Hellenists (in Jerusalem); but they were attempting to kill him. When the believers learned of it, they brought him down to Caesarea and sent him off to Tarsus" Acts 9:29-30.

Our story picks up in Acts 11:19. The story is about the church in Antioch. The characteristics of this church are so compelling they call for a close look. Keep in mind that Saul had a huge influence in this church. Consider eight characteristics of the church derived from the scripture for this study. Rather than elaborate on the characteristics, it should be an interesting activity for you and/or your group to search for the is evidence of these strong traits. Maybe it will help with your memory of them if the first four characteristics begin with the letter E. Feel free to change any of the words and find additional traits.

EVANGELISTIC is the first. That is, they were proclaiming their faith. Note that these folks were probably new believers and not apostles.

EDUCATIONAL: the people were eager to learn more about the scripture and living as people who followed Jesus, the Christ. Did you note the teacher? Who enlisted the teacher?

ETHICAL may be hidden in one word, so here is a hint. They were called Christians, first in Antioch. Some think the word was used in derision toward them, but even so the word carries the idea of living Christ like.

ELIOMOSINARY means benevolent. I use it because of the E, but it was a new word to me. Do you see evidence that the church was generous? Sound sort of Jesus like?

WORSHIP probably should be placed at the head of the list. It is in worship that persons give thanks, forgive and are forgiven, praise God. Add to the list and find the scripture reference.

MISSION OR MISHIONAL the idea of outreach and spreading the good news to all.

INCLUSIVE: love was extended to ALL. Did you notice the diversity of person in the list in Acts: 13:1?

Application to Life

The first application is to do the study as suggested above. Next think about how Saul may have influenced any or all the characteristics and why you think so.

Compare the Antioch church to yourself and then to your church or study group.

Where is improvement needed and what are you and/or your group going to do about it.

Paul's First Missionary Journey
Acts 13:2-52; 14:1-28

Barnabas and Saul, set apart by the church at Antioch, began what is called Paul's first missionary journey. Notice, Barnabas is named first. They take with them John Mark, a young man from Jerusalem, who was related to Barnabas. See Colossians 4:10. They went first to the island of Cyprus, Barnabas' home country, See Acts 4:36.

Passing through the island they came to Paphos. There they meet two men: a Jewish false prophet and magician named Bar Jesus or Elymas; and proconsul named Sergius Paulus. Sergius was very interested in Saul's message, but was hindered by Elymas. It was at this point that Luke, author of Acts, began to use Saul's Greek name Paul. Paul announced to Elymas that he would be blinded because of his interference. And so, he was. Recall Paul's blindness led to his conversion, we are not told what became of Elymas. But Sergius became a believer.

Paul and company went next to Perga in Pamphylia, at which point John Mark parted company and returned to his home in Jerusalem. We will return to this event in Acts 15.36.

Next stop was Antioch in Pisidia. As was their custom, they went to the synagogue on the Sabbath. They were offered an opportunity to speak, He reminds them of their Jewish history and that God had sent Jesus to fulfill his promises. Some believed, but some stirred up trouble and drove Paul and Barnabas out of town.

A similar welcome and then persecution occurred in Iconium. So, to avoid stoning, they fled to Lystra. One of their listeners there was a man born crippled. Paul called on the man to stand, he did and was healed. The people were so amazed they call Barnabas, Zeus and Paul, Hermes, because he was the main speaker. The apostles had to explain that they were not gods, but men who brought good news that the God of all creation would fill their hearts with joy. But Jews from Antioch came, won over the crowd and stoned Paul, leaving him for dead.

Paul survived and the day after, he and Barnabas continued to Derbe.

Understanding, courage and compassion for the new believers led them to return to the cities where they had preached to strengthen the believers. That they did on their way back to Antioch, the church that sent them out. Application to Life

How does your church spread the good news both near and far? How do you participate?

In what ways might you and your church be a hindrance to those who are seeking for life's answers? Surely not an Elymas, but it can happen without being a magician or meaning to be a false prophet.

You would not want to stone someone with whom you disagree, but are there ways you mistreat people who believe and live differently than you? Take time to discuss and write out the answers to these questions. Also list ways you can improve your witness.

Part 2

Paul's Second Missionary Journey

(A.D.50-52)

Paul and Barnabas Separated
Acts 15:36-40

Introduction

Whether or not you studied part one of The Life and Ministry of the Apostle Paul, this is a good time to be reminded of several important facts about the Book of Acts and some clues that will help you understand part 2 of this study.

Acts is believed to have been written by Luke, a physician, whom you will learn more about in session number 3 of Part 2. Luke also wrote the Gospel of Luke. Compare Luke 1:1-2 and Acts 1:1-2, both books have the same author and recipient. Both books give a strong emphasis to prayer, Holy Spirit, the poor and a high regard for women.

Some translations of the Bible entitle Acts as The Acts of the Apostles. If you have read the book of Acts, you might think that a better title might be Acts of Paul and a Few Other Apostles, or Acts of Holy Spirit, or Acts of the Early Church. What title would you give this book? Read Acts 1:1-2 and consider the implication that Luke is going to tell of the "Continuing Acts of Jesus."

One other reminder concerns Judaism. Remember Jesus was a Jew. He read and studied Hebrew Scripture (the Christian Old Testament). He attended Synagogue and worshipped at the Temple in Jerusalem. He fulfilled the law. Paul was also a Jew and did the same things. Consider this, was Jesus or Paul trying to begin a new religion called Christianity or were they attempting to show how to relate to God who is love, by being a loving and inclusive, nonjudgmental people?

Now read Acts 15:36-41. Remember Paul, Barnabas and John Mark had made the first missionary journey referred to in these verses. So, in this study Paul proposed a plan, Barnabas presents a problem, and both determine a solution.

Paul Presents a Plan for a Second Journey

Paul's proposal was to return to the same places they had been on the first journey in order to see how the followers of Jesus were doing and to encourage them. A wonderful idea, don't you think? Paul and Barnabas had seen many persons accept "the Way" of Jesus. But Paul knew that if they followed Jesus' teachings and way of life they would run into trouble. They would need their presence and words of encouragement. Remember, Barnabas name meant son of encouragement. This is as true today as then. New and longtime followers of Jesus need the fellowship of other disciples. That is a major purpose of the church. It is to be a gathering for sharing, instructing, fellowship and worship.

Barnabas Presents a Problem

Barnabas thought the second journey and purpose was a great idea. He was ready to go, but he wanted to take John Mark. Recall John Mark was a young man from Jerusalem. On the first journey he "quit" and returned home. Was he ill? Maybe homesick? Could he have been frightened? Whatever the reason he left them and returned home. So, Paul is unwilling for Mark to go with them. But Barnabas insists. John Mark seems to have been his cousin, see Colossian 4:10. The problem caused the two missionaries to part company.

The Solution Doubles the Work

So, Barnabas took with him John Mark and they go back to Cyprus. Cyprus was Barnabas home country and was the first stop on the first missionary journey. By the way, John Mark is the writer of the Gospel of Mark. Also read Colossians 4:10 and Second Timothy 4:11 to see Paul's later feeling about Mark. Everyone needs a Barnabas who gives second chances, don't you think? Paul took Silas with him and traveled by land on the second journey.

Application to Life

Whether you are a new follower of Jesus or have been one for a long time, you need the encouragement of friend(s). Think about and discuss ways you can encourage others. Do you know someone who needs a "second chance?" You may want to discuss how friends can disagree and not harm their friendship. Do you find that doing a difficult act of mercy or witness is easier if done with a friend? Do you think that is why Paul took Silas and Barnabas took Mark? Pray for opportunities to tell others about how God loves them, and Jesus calls them to be his disciples.

Prayer: *Lord, help us to be loving in our ways that others will follow Jesus. Amen*

Paul and Silas and Letter of Galatians
Acts 15:36-41 & Galatians

Introduction

Paul and Barnabas agree to make a return visit to the churches of their first journey, but strongly disagree about taking John Mark, who had deserted them on the first journey. So, Paul takes Silas via land to Galatia and Barnabas and Mark go to Cyprus.

Be aware that in the Acts stories Paul is the major character, but this is only part of the early church story and mission work. Read Acts 2:5-12 to refresh your memory that more than fifteen different countries were represented at the Pentecost event. Many believed Jesus to be the Messiah and returned to their homes to tell others. Read Acts 8:1-2 and 11:19-21. In chapter 8, Philip preaches in Samaria and baptizes an Egyptian official. Thomas is believed to have gone to India. The point is, a lot more was taking place than what is recorded in Acts.

In the texts for this study we follow Paul and Silas to churches in Asia Minor and look at his opposition and response in his Letter to the Galatians believers.

Paul and Silas Return to Encourage the Churches

As noted in the last study, the idea of returning to encourage was from the Spirit of God. New and old followers of Jesus need to be taught and encouraged. They will have temptations, problems, and suffering. Following Jesus does not exempt one from life but demands participation in life. The participation is often counter to the culture in which a believer lives. That requires courage and love. The great temptation is to conform and accept injustice and structural evil. "Everybody is doing it," becomes an excuse to live an unexamined life. Paul's message was Jesus coming in flesh, living a life of love, dying because of sin, defeating death in the resurrection, thus revealing to the ultimate that God loves his whole creation. Salvation is a gift of grace. Salvation is responding to that grace in a love relationship to God and others.

Paul's Enemies Had Followed and Contradicted Him

Like Jesus, Paul had those who did not accept his idea of God receiving any and all based on a faith relationship. These enemies of Paul were called Judaizers. They were Jewish Christians who believed that a non-Jew could only be Christian if they kept Jewish law, especially circumcision. They were also questioning Paul's claim to be an apostle. It was believed an apostle had to have seen Jesus. Paul claimed that in his conversion experience he saw Jesus. Read Acts 9.

Paul Warned the Galatian Believers with a Letter

At this point in the study read at least the first chapter of Galatians. It would be better to read the whole letter. It will take only a short time. Some of it will be hard to grasp. But you will easily get the heart of Paul's argument.

Did you note the fierce emotion in the letter? Paul seems angry, maybe a righteous indignation. There is too much for this study, but the summary is: salvation, relating rightly with God and other human beings, is based on God's grace, free gift. It is an experience of faith, not keeping rules. The Judaizers wanted to turn the religion into a merit, rule keeping, appeasing God labor. Paul contended that in Jesus you see God as loving. All are saved by God's grace. Abraham knew that relationship before the law was given. The law is good to show wrong. But to live with love surpasses law.

"You are all sons (and daughters) of God through faith in Christ Jesus, for all of you who were baptized into Christ have clothed yourselves with Christ. There is neither Jew nor Greek, slave nor free, male nor female, for you are all one in Christ Jesus." 3:26-28. You have been set free to become servants of the Spirit of God. And those controlled by God's Spirit bear fruit of "love, joy, peace, patience, kindness, goodness, faithfulness, gentleness and self-control. Against such things there is no law." 5:22-23. Paul then ends the letter with a prayer for grace to be with their spirit.

Application to Life

A basic belief of a Christian should be freedom of conscience. Over the years organized religion has used rules and fear to control people. The law of Christ is to love. Love fulfills the other "laws." Can you think of rules or beliefs used to control persons through doubt and fear? Take time to meditate on each of the fruit of the Spirit. How are you practicing each of these? Note how positive and practical they are. You might want to determine to purposefully practice these in your relationships at home and in society.

Prayer: *Dear God, may I be led by your Spirit today to produce fruit of your Spirit. Amen*

Paul and Silas in Derbe, Lystra
Acts 15:40-41; 16:1-5

Introduction

The apostle Paul was a dynamic, over powering character, as you may have already decided. He was the kind of person who would be considered by most standards as very independent, self-sufficient. In fact, Paul's name is on thirteen books of the New Testament and most of Acts is about him. So, over half the pages of the New Testament are attributed to him. But you may want to review or reread Luke's words about Paul in Acts 9 and 15. Consider making a list of the people who helped Paul. Check Acts 22:3 to learn that Paul had a famous Jewish teacher named Gamaliel. Ananias was of assistance in 9:10-19 and Barnabas stood up for him when the church in Jerusalem was afraid to receive him 9:26-30.

Now, read Acts 15:40 -16:5, for this study of Paul and Silas going back to visit the followers of Jesus in Lystra and Derbe. If you go back to the first missionary journey you will recall that Paul was beaten and left for dead at Lystra. But he revived and went back into the city. How brave is that? Now, he was returning. It was here that he called Timothy to join the missionary team. Timothy became a major partner of Paul. Paul gave Timothy a pattern for team work.

Paul Asked Timothy to Join the Team

Timothy had probably met Paul on his first visit to Lystra. Timothy had a Greek father and a Jewish mother named

Eunice and grandmother named Lois (I Timothy 1:5). These two ladies taught the Hebrew Bible (Old Testament) to Timothy. So as a young man, probably on Paul's first journey, Timothy became a Jesus follower.

Paul had Timothy circumcised because he was Jewish. This is a reminder that Paul was not anti-Jewish or anti law. And so, Timothy goes with Paul and Silas as they leave the Derbe, Lystra area.

Timothy Became a Major Member of the Team

Paul lists Timothy as a co-author of six of his letters. Read the first verse(s) of II Corinthians, Philippians, Colossians, I & II Thessalonians and Philemon. Paul wrote two letters to Timothy, I & II Timothy. Timothy became a dependable messenger for Paul to other churches, I Corinthians 4:17 and I Thessalonians 3:2-6. Read of Timothy's close relationship and presence with Paul through thick and thin, even when Paul was in prison and being forsaken by some of his team members, Philippians 2:19; Colossians 1:1 and Romans 16:21. If you have a Bible Dictionary or Bible Concordance, look up Timothy. Read Paul's I & II Timothy for more on the Paul – Timothy relationship.

Paul Gave Timothy a Pattern for Team Building

"You then, my son, be strong in the grace that is in Christ Jesus. And the things you have heard me say in the presence of many witnesses entrust to reliable men who will also be qualified to teach others" II Timothy 2:1-2. See how Paul practiced what he taught? He is asking Timothy to do exactly as he was doing when he chose and taught Timothy. An abundance of advice, warnings and help for him in the letters.

Application to Life

Give some serious thought to the importance of teaching children. Timothy from a very early age was taught. Be careful to keep teaching on the child's level of understanding. There are so many wonderful things a child can learn about living that adults seem to have missed: God loves all people regardless of race, religion, nationality, be truthful, honest, kind, generous, compassionate. Add to this list.

"No man is an island," not even Paul. We need each other. Think about how you can cooperate with other persons and groups in doing ministry and missions.

Prayer: *Lord Jesus, help me to be a faithful team member in your ministry. Amen.*

Paul's Call to Europe
Acts 16:6-10

Introduction

Do you think that God speaks to you in different ways and means? He speaks in and through scripture. That may be why you are doing these Bible studies. He speaks through nature, his creation, read Psalm 8 and 19 and Romans 1:20. He may speak to you through other persons' words and acts. Jesus told his disciples that Holy Spirit would be in them and teach them, John 14:25-26. What about dreams and circumstances? Look for these two in this study of Acts 16:6-10.

Paul had a plan for his journey. In fact, he had a backup plan. His plans were forbidden. God had another plan. Recall from a previous study, a suggestion was made to keep a list of those enlisted to be on Paul's missionary team. A new one will be added in this study.

Paul Had a Journey Plan

Did you note in reading that he planned to go into northern Galatia and was forbidden? He then decided to go northwest into Bithynia and was forbidden by the Spirit of Jesus. How did the Spirit speak to him? What is meant here? How did he know? Could it have been circumstances? Many believe that Paul had a disease that may have been made worse had he gone north. The idea is that sometimes conditions and circumstances may be used by God to direct lives.

However, Paul got the message, he accepted that those two doors were closed to him. But God opened another door for Paul and his team. Paul Was Given a Different Journey Plan At night, in a dream, Paul saw a man of Macedonia crying out to him, "Come over to Macedonia and help us." Paul took that to be God's way of saying that they should cross over into Europe. Macedonia was named for Philip of Macedon, the father of Alexandra the Great. Some would compare Alexandra's desire to conquer the world with Paul's desire to tell the Good News to the whole world.

So, Paul and His team determined to cross over and proclaim the Good News to the Macedonians (next lesson). There is an old gospel hymn with these lines: We have heard the Macedonian call today, Send the light! Send the light!

You may want to sing this with your group.

Paul Was Given a New Team Member, Luke

God always gives graciously. The new team member was Luke, a physician and the writer of the books of Luke and Acts. How is this known? Reread 16:10.

Up to this point Luke had written in the third person pronoun "they" did or went, etc. In verse 10 he uses the first-person pronoun "we." So, if Luke wrote the book, he must be in the "we." Now the team consists of Paul, Silas, Timothy and doctor Luke.

Do you find it wonderfully fascinating that Luke, a doctor and writer, "just happened" to join with the ailing apostle and be with him much, if not all, Paul's remaining years? Read Colossians 4:10-14. This indicates that Luke was there at the prison to minister to Paul.

Paul wrote in Romans 8:28, "And we know that in all things God works for the good of those who love him." Do you think Paul had experiences like the ones in this study in mind when he wrote that?

Application to Life

Look for the will of God in the circumstances that surround your life. How may God be speaking to you. Keep in mind that your abilities, possessions, and relationships are ways that God may be speaking to you of how, when and where you are to serve. Knowing God's will in the circumstances of life is a matter of prayer and discussion with trusted friends and family. Prayer: May your Spirit direct our words and actions this day, dear Lord. Amen.

Paul and Companions in Philippi: Lydia, the First Convert in Europe
Acts 16:11-15

Introduction

In an earlier study some recurring themes in Luke's writing of his Gospel and Acts were mentioned. Do you remember any of them? Refresh your memory: work of **Holy Spirit**; God's love and care for **the poor and outcasts** of society; importance of **prayer;** value of **women; and inclusiveness,** that is, God's love for all people and his creation. Keep looking for these in the travels of Paul and his team. Chapter 16 is filled with them. In the last study (16:1-10), Paul had a dream or vision in which a man from Macedonia was calling him to come over and help them. The team had decided that was the guidance of Holy Spirit and they crossed the Aegean Sea into Macedonia and Europe. They docked at Neapolis, sea port for Philippi. They traveled the few miles to Philippi. Paul found a prayer meeting. Lydia and her house accepted Jesus as Messiah. Lydia offered lodging for Paul and his companions.

Paul Found a Prayer Meeting

Philippi was a colony of Rome. The residents included several retired Roman soldiers. It was very much a Roman city in population and culture. That may be the reason that it seemed to have no synagogue. Remember, on the first journey Paul had a habit of going first to the synagogue in the cities he visited. He went there to convince Jews and Gentile "God fearers" that Jesus was truly the Jewish Messiah. Recall, a synagogue was the Jewish place of worship and study.

Some way Paul learned that there was a prayer group meeting outside town by the river. So, on the Sabbath, he and his companions Silas, Timothy and Luke find the group. It is a group of women. They can sit with the group and Paul tells them about Jesus. Lydia seems to be the leader of the group and a worshipper of God. She was Asian, from Thyatira. At some point, a church was established there (Rev. 2:19). Lydia was a business woman, a dealer in purple cloth. Was she in Philippi on business? Did she have two homes, one in Philippi and one in Thyatira? Lydia Became a Follower of Jesus Lydia's heart was opened by God to hear Paul's message. She and all her household were baptized Luke did not tell who and how many made up her household. Did she have a husband, children, servants? She seems to have been wealthy to have a house with room for four guests. Did she feed them also? This is the beginning of the church at Philippi. Paul will later write one of his most cherished letters to that church. You might want to stop here and read the short letter. Many calls it a letter of joy. It is a letter of joy, calling for unity in the church and urging them to depend upon God to supply all their needs. It has several verses that you may want to commit to memory. It was also a letter of thanksgiving. The folk at Philippi more than once sent offerings to assist with Paul's work. They must have been some of his favorite folk.

So, the charter members of that group were Lydia, a well to do woman and her household. Watch for diversity of membership as you do the next two studies.

Application to Life

Are you in a prayer/ study group? Maybe you should begin one or join one in your church. Does place matter as to worship and study? The ladies met by the river. Is there advantage of walking, studying, meditating outdoors? Are women accepted in your group? As in some of the other studies, prejudices and preconceived ideas about various kinds of people need to be examined. Does God really expect you to love those "others?" Hospitality is another Bible theme. Think about your own ideas of being hospitable and being the recipient of the hospitality of others. Prayer: Lord, give us the joy of being open to others. Amen.

Paul and Companions in Philippi; The Slave Girl
Acts 16:16-18

Introduction

Have you been noticing how Paul's ministry compared to that of Jesus? Recall Luke, in Acts 1:1, indicated that he had written to Theophilus (lover of God) about what Jesus had been doing (Gospel of Luke) and infers that he is about to write what Jesus continued/continues to do (Acts). For starters both Jesus and Paul preached the Good News (gospel) that God loves all people. They both began at the synagogue, but had no problem preaching where ever any one would listen. Jesus and Paul taught, healed and cast out "evil spirits." Both were led by the Spirit of God. They both got in trouble because of their counter cultural words and actions. They were criticized for religious, civil, and economic disturbance of the status quo. Watch, especially, in this and the following studies. The comparisons will continue to the end of Acts. Consider how Paul continued worshiping by the river; how a possessed slave girl followed each day; and how Paul healed her.

Paul Continued to Worship by the River

In the last study Paul and his companions (Silas, Timothy and Luke) had found a group of believers in God who held prayer meetings by the river, outside the city gate. Paul spoke to the ladies and some believed that Jesus was the promised Jewish Messiah. Lydia, a well to do lady, was one of them. She invited

Paul and his group to stay in her house. They did. And her whole household was baptized.

It seems that their river prayer meeting continued to be a daily ritual. Try to imagine Paul and his group, along with Lydia, her household, and the other ladies making their way to the river each day. Do you think others noticed and followed? It seems likely that could have happened. Perhaps the original group of ladies made an effort to get others to join them to hear Paul's teaching. Well, for sure one lady or girl followed. That leads to the second section of this study.

A Possessed Girl Followed Paul

There are numerous ethical issues to deal with in these verses. The girl was a slave, owned by men (how many owners?). She was possessed by the spirit of pythonos. Python was the guard of the oracle at Delphi. So there is a different religious element. The men were using, prostituting, the slave girl's ability to make predictions. She was an economic item, not a person, to them. Keep all this in mind for discussion in Applications to Life at the end of the study. What the girl said or shouted as she followed Paul and his companions was true. They were slaves of the most high God and did bring a way of salvation. Do you find it fascinating who recognized the truth and who in the next study will make lying accusations to protect their economic interests?

Paul Healed the Girl

The girl's following and shouting had gone on for days. Paul became annoyed and exorcized the spirit. What about her annoyed Paul? It could have been any of the problems listed above. The fact that she had such a spirit, that she was a slave, that she was being used, that she was considered worthless except for making money for her owners. Give some thought to this picture. How do you think you would have felt? What do you think bothered Paul the most? Do you find it interesting that the story does not tell what the girl did after she was set free of the spirit of python? Did she leave her owners? Did she go with Lydia's group and join the prayer meeting? You would hope so. If so, note the contrast. Lydia is of the upper wealthy class in society and the girl a slave. The point? God loves and accepts all as his children.

Application to Life

Do you realize that slave trade is rampant in the world today? Check your computer or go to your library and check on this. Thousands of children and adults are bought and sold like things. They are used and abused in most demeaning ways. There are organizations given to the task of setting these people free. What is being done where you live? Should you check to see if your clothes or food is produced by slave labor? Is your church open to people from all "classes" in society?

Prayer: *Father, help us to help free those in slavery and use our freedom wisely. Amen*

Paul and Companions in Philippi: The Philippian Jailer
Acts 16:19-40

Introduction

In the previous study (Acts 16:16-18), Paul and Silas had healed a slave girl who was used by her owners to make money by fortune telling. The owners became very angry. This story would make a great drama in seven scenes.

Scene 1. Paul and Silas were Arrested, verses 19-21

Would you call this a citizen's arrest? When the owners saw that the girl was healed of her "divination possession," their hope of money making with her was gone. They dragged Paul and Silas before the city authorities and charged them with teaching things unlawful for Romans to do. Does this remind you of events in Jesus life? People get very upset when their corrupt ways of making money are hindered. Does this happen in your culture's business and government? Note that the slave girl is not mentioned, or specific charges made. Men with money can incite the crowds.

Scene 2. Paul and Silas were Beaten and Jailed verses 2-24

The magistrates or city authorities have Paul and Silas stripped and beaten. They are jailed and put in stocks. They are placed in an "inner" cell. Why do you suppose there was this extra precaution taken? Isn't it interesting how something new or change brings fear to those who are insecure? Did you notice there was no testimony or defense registered by Paul and Silas? Were they not given an opportunity to answer the charges?

Scene 3. Paul and Silas Sang and Prayed. verses 25-26

There is an old saying," He sang up a storm." Well that happened there. At midnight, wrongly accused, beaten and in stocks, Paul and Silas sang and prayed. The whole jail was shaken by an earthquake. Doors flew open, chains and stocks fell off. When the jailer, shaken awake, saw what had happened, he feared for his life. He must have felt sure that his prisoners had escaped. The law would require his life for their escape. He ran with sword in hand, ready to kill himself if the prisoners were gone. But he found them all there. Paul told him not to worry.

Scene 4. The Jailer's Fear Turned to Awe verses 27-32

For the jailer the prisoners being there was a miracle. He brought Paul and Silas out and asked, "What must I do to be saved?" They replied, "Believe in the Lord Jesus and you will be saved – you and your household." What a turn of events! Can you visualize the jailer and those in his house bowing in thanksgiving at the recognition of Jesus as their Lord? Do you think there might have been more praying and singing?

Scene 5. Washing, Feeding and Rejoicing. verses 33-34

Rejoicing could certainly include singing and praying. The point of this scene is to show the change in the jailer. He washed the wounds of the prisoners and fed them. Are these not signs of a changed heart? Faith acts. Think of the courage that the jailer now had. Will he be disciplined for his kindness to the prisoners? What answer will he give for doing what he did?

Scene 6. Paul and Silas Faced the Authorities verses 35-39

This scene is courageously humorous. Word was sent for the jailer to release Paul and Silas. They refused to leave the jail. They sent word to the city authorities that they must come and escort them out. They were. without trial, beaten and jailed as Roman citizens. Now, who is afraid? They come and beg Paul and Silas to leave town.

Scene 7. Paul and Silas Said Farewell to the Believers of Philippi verse 40

Paul and Silas go to Lydia's home and bid farewell to those followers of Jesus. They depart for Thessalonica. Picture the joy and sadness that must have been in all their hearts. Application to Life

Compare this story with that of Peter's jail experience in Acts 5:12-32.; Note the "classes" of followers of Jesus in Philippi: Lydia a wealthy lady; the salve girl; and a "middle class" jailer and family. Inclusive, God loves all. Have your group rewrite this "drama" and perform it.

Prayer: *Lord, Give us courage to face the trials of life as your followers. Amen.*

Paul And Silas In Thessalonica
Acts 17:1-15

Introduction

Have you been following Paul's journey on a Bible map? If not, look in the back of your Bible or a Bible Dictionary for a map. It will help you visualize the distance Paul and his companions traveled. Find Lystra, Philippi, and Thessalonica. Now read the text for this study, Acts 17:1-15. Paul and his companions fled from Philippi. They went through Amphipolis, Apollonia, to Thessalonica. They traveled about 100 miles. Thessalonica was a major city. The Egnatian Way, a main Roman road to the east, ran through the city. The city was built by Casandra in 325 B.C. and named for his wife who was daughter of Philip of Macedon. She was Alexandra's half-sister. In this study note the preaching and persecution of Paul in Thessalonica and then in Berea.

Paul and Silas Preached in Thessalonica

Paul and Silas went to the Jewish synagogue to tell fellow Jews that Jesus is the Messiah. They used the Hebrew Scripture, the Christian Old Testament, to argue that Jesus had to suffer and rise from the dead. It would be interesting to know what scriptures he used. They taught on three consecutive Sabbath days. Many God-fearing Greeks and prominent women believed.

But, as in the other cities, there were those who were jealous and caused trouble. In this study some Jews enlisted ruffians from the market place to cause a riot. They intended to bring

Paul before the civil authorities. When he could not be found, they drug his host, Jason, into court. He was accused of housing Paul and his friends. But Jason could post bail and go free.

The charge was that Paul was claiming that there was another king, Jesus. Is this not the same charge brought against Jesus? See John 19:15. Mob violence is nothing new. Jesus and Paul met it. It often, as with them, started because someone's religion, politics or economics is threatened. The Jews were jealous about religious beliefs, the slave owner in the previous study was upset because his money making was disturbed. The city leaders did not want to upset the status quo. Their vocation was also threatened. Paul and Silas were sent away that night. They went to Berea.

Paul and Silas in Berea

Berea was about sixty miles from Thessalonica. Again, they found a synagogue and could teach that Jesus is the suffering, resurrected Messiah. "Now the Bereans were of more noble character than the Thessalonians, for they received the message with great eagerness and examined the Scriptures every day to see if what Paul said was true" verse 11. There are great lessons here. One is that Paul was using the Hebrew Scripture to drive home the truth about Jesus. Two, the people did their own study to see for themselves. Bible study is important, that is why you are doing this study. What you think is important. God can speak to you through the Scriptures. It is good to have a teacher, but you also need to study. For the Jews, the Scripture may have more than one meaning. That is still true. The good news: many Jews, Greek men and women believed. The bad news: trouble makers arrived from Thessalonica to continue their persecution.

Paul was sent off to Athens, but Silas and Timothy remained in Berea. This may indicate that Paul was the primary target for persecution. The next study will be Paul Alone in Athens (Acts 17:16-34). This passage deserves several readings. Application to Life

How open are you to seek or listen to new truth and other interpretations of Scripture? How does culture affect your beliefs? How could your religious beliefs, economics, or political ideologies prevent you from accepting new truth? How has culture shaped these aspects of your life? Discuss how difficult it would be to love one who does you harm. What can you do to share your belief in Jesus? Think about to whom, when, how and why you should share your beliefs. Are you willing to listen to religious stories and experiences of others? Why not ask persons from other denominations and religions to talk with your group?

Prayer: *Dear Father, help us to be faithful and loving in our witness. Amen*

Paul Alone in Athens
Acts 17:16-34

Introduction

What do you know about Greek philosophy? Athens was the center for Greek culture and philosophy. In this study Paul was in Athens. He was there to avoid more persecution that had plagued him in Philippi, Thessalonica and Berea. He had left Silas and Timothy in Berea, probably to continue teaching the folk there who had been so receptive to the Scripture study. Read the text for this study, Acts 17:16-34. Watch for the philosophical curiosity of the Athenians; note Paul's method of teaching; and consider the results.

Paul Observed the Philosophical Curiosity of the Athenians

Paul saw statues and other objects in Athens which he called idols. They said Paul was speaking of foreign gods when he preached to them about Jesus' resurrection. Two schools of thought are mentioned. Epicurus founded his school about 310 B.C. Some of the beliefs were: happiness is the goal of life; the world was created by constant movement of atoms; gods exist but had nothing to do with people; religious rules and rituals were useless and unnecessary. Zeno was founder of the Stoics about 300 B.C. They were committed to inner freedom and devotion to duty; virtue was the ultimate good; and human reason was the same as divine reason that governed all.

Because of their seeking for truth, the Athenians were eager to listen to Paul. In fact, they brought him to the Areopagus to speak. The Areopagus was both a place known as Mars Hill and a council of some 30 learned men. Do you think that this gave Paul a great opportunity to speak? He was able to teach in the synagogue of Athens and to speak to the philosophers. Paul Spoke to the Areopagus What do you think of Paul's opening statement? Reread 17:22-23.

See how he began where they were? He complimented them for being very religious. He spoke to them about one of their icons, an altar to an unknown god. This opened the door for Paul to say, "Let me tell you who that God is."

God is creator of all that exists. He is self-sufficient. He has given to humans; life, breath and everything else. He created all nations and gave them their place. God desires human kind to seek him. In God we live, move, and have our being. Paul quotes a Greek poet, "We are his off spring" verse 28. Was Paul asking these people to recognize that God loves them all? Was he saying that: Jesus' life, death and resurrection mean, "This is how much God loves you?"

If this is so, then they need not make and worship idols. There will be a final judgment and God desires all mankind to change their minds about God. He is neither wood, nor stone, nor a tyrant, but a loving parent calling all to come home.

The People Responded

The result of Paul's speech to the Areopagus was mixed. Some sneered because they did not believe in a resurrection. Some had their curiosity stirred enough to ask for another meeting with Paul. Some became believers and followers of Jesus. One was Dionysius, who was a member of the Areopagus. Another was Damaris, a woman. There were others, verse 34. This may mean a number of women, for at the beginning of verse 34: "A few men became followers of Paul." Paul then went to Corinth. That is the next study Acts 18:1-22.

Application to Life

Discuss how you might use Paul's complimentary, non-condemning approach in discussing Jesus with others.

Do you think Paul had knowledge of Greek philosophy? Was it a help to him in talking with the Greeks? Is it important that you know what others believe in order to discuss with them what you believe? Should your group do a study of comparative religions? Does God love all of his creation, including people of other cultures, races, and religions?

Prayer: *Lord, Guide our thoughts, words and actions toward those unlike us. Amen*

Paul in Corinth and Return to Antioch
Acts 18:1-22

Introduction

Do you think cities have personalities? Maybe that isn't the right word, but, think about the last few places Paul had been on his second missionary journey. Then compare them to Corinth where this study begins. In Acts 16 Paul was in Philippi, a colony of Rome and inhabited by many retired soldiers. It may have been like a little Rome. Thessalonica was a booming commercial town on the Egnatian Way. Berea's people were described as "more noble" in character than those in Thessalonica. Athens was the cultural and philosophical center of Greece.

This study is about Paul's eighteen months in Corinth.

Corinth was a seaman's town with all the "sin" that goes with it. It was on an isthmus about five miles wide. The Saronic Gulf was on one side and the Gulf of Corinth on the other. Ships would send their cargo by land from one gulf to the other to avoid the dangers via Malea. They passed through Corinth, making it a large commercial center. Corinth could be called a synonym for debauchery.

Observe, Paul preached in synagogues and houses; he found new companions in work and ministry; and he completed his second missionary journey. Paul Preached in Synagogues and Houses Remember, Paul was a Jew. He went first to Jewish synagogues to preach. He taught from a Jewish (Hebrew) Bible. His message of good news was that Jesus was the long expected Jewish Messiah (Christ). Paul followed this pattern in Corinth. Crispus, the synagogue leader, became a believer. Some other Jews were upset, and Paul had to leave the synagogue, but went next door and began preaching to Gentiles. He may have used the home of Aquila and Pricilla.

Paul's opponents took their case against him to a civil leader named Gallio. The charge was similar to that in previous cities. Gallio would have nothing to do with their dispute over religion and dismissed the case. You might think of how religions in your area want to use civil power for favors to themselves and rejection or harm to other religions.

Paul Met New Companions in Work and Ministry

If you have been doing the preceding studies in the series, you have noted that in nearly every place Paul adds companions to his ministry and journey. In Corinth he met Aquila and his wife Pricilla. They had recently had to leave Rome on the order of the emperor and had come to Corinth. They were Jews and it is unknown if they were Christian Jews before meeting Paul. They, like Paul, were tent makers or leather workers. Paul both worked and lived with them. Recall Lydia in Philippi?

They might have had a tent and leather shop on a street in Corinth. There they could meet and witness to all kinds of people. When Silas and Timothy rejoined Paul after their stay in Macedonia, Paul may have given full time to teaching. He was adamant about not receiving pay for his preaching. Read I Thessalonians 2:9 and II Thessalonians 3:8. Do you think the believers in Philippi sent Paul a gift by Silas and Timothy? Read Philippians 4:15-19.

After a year and half of work there were many believers in Corinth. But that group had many problems. Read the letters that Paul later wrote to them, I and II Corinthians. You will see that churches have those same problems today. Speaking of Paul's letters. He may have written I and II Thessalonians from Corinth.

Paul Completed His Second Missionary Journey

Paul was eager to get back to Antioch. He made several stops on the way. He leaves Aquila and Pricilla in Ephesus. There will be more about that church on Paul's third journey. He sailed to Caesarea and went up to Jerusalem before going to Antioch, the church that had sent him on the journey. Did you note Paul's making a vow and having his head shaved? Paul, a Jew, who believed Jesus was the Christ.

Application to Life

Read I Corinthians to get a better idea of Corinth, the people, the believers and their problems. Make a list of the problems. You should find at least ten. Which of the problems do you and your church have? How can you and your group work to correct the problems?

Think about and discuss the Jews trying to get state or civil courts to punish Paul. Does that happen today in your area? What can be done about it?

Today Paul would be called a bi-vocational preacher. He worked to earn a living and did his preaching free of charge.

He, later in his writing, makes a case for providing for ministers. Discuss the use and abuse of church finances.

Prayer: *Lord, Help us to use our opportunities for ministry and finances wisely. Amen*

Part 3

Paul's Third Missionary Journey

53-57A.D.

Paul at Ephesus
Acts 18:23-28; 19:1-20)

(I Corinthians written during his two years there)

Introduction

Luke, believed to be the author of Acts, begins and covers at least several weeks of ministry in just one verse. Stop here and read Acts 18:23. Paul began his third missionary journey by land as he did his second journey. He went to visit and encourage the churches in Galatia and Phrygia. Luke did not take time to name the churches, nor what Paul said or did to encourage them. Did he go to Iconium, Lystra and Derbe? The emphasis seems to be to get to Ephesus. That is where this study takes place. Now, read the entire passage Acts 18:23-28; 19:1-20. Look for: Paul's encounter with disciples of John the Baptist; Paul's moved from the synagogue to a lecture hall; and the miracles God worked through Paul.

Paul Encountered Disciples of John the Baptist

Before Paul gets to Ephesus a man named Apollos arrived from Alexandria, Egypt. He was a Jewish Christian, knowledgeable of the Hebrew Scripture and an eloquent speaker. But he knew only the baptism of John. Aquila and Pricilla, whom Paul had left in Ephesus (Acts 18:19), instructed Apollos more fully about the Way. The Way had become a name for the followers of Jesus, Jewish or Gentile. What do you think they told him? Maybe the same thing Paul told the group he discovered in Ephesus who had not heard of the Holy Spirit.

When Paul got to Ephesus, he found a group of about twelve believers who had only received the baptism of John. They said they had not heard of the Holy Spirit. Could the difference in the teaching and baptism of John and that of Jesus followers have to do with present and future tense? John was calling for repentance (change of mind and direction) looking forward to the coming of the Messiah, Jesus. Jesus' followers were proclaiming that Jesus was the Messiah and that Jesus was present in them through Holy Spirit. So, it became a matter of recognition and realization for Apollos and the group Paul found in Ephesus. The Spirit of God was in them. They were given signs of the Spirit's presence like those experienced in Acts 2:4.

Paul Taught in the Synagogue and Public Lecture Hall

For three months Paul taught in the Jewish synagogue. He taught them about the kingdom of God. Remember this was a major topic in the teaching of Jesus. The four gospels had not been written, but surely Paul knew a lot of the teaching of Jesus through his time with Peter, James and other of Jesus' disciples. Some of the Jews did not agree with Paul and he had to leave the synagogue. He used the lecture hall of Tyrannus for two years. "So, all the Jews and Greeks who lived in the province of Asia heard the word of the Lord" (19:10). Luke may be using hyperbole here, meaning many heard.

God Worked Miracles Through Paul

People were being healed in the name of Jesus. Some magic workers desired the gift that Paul had for commercial reasons, that is greed. They tried to heal in the name of Jesus. It failed in what could be considered a comical way. The man is not healed but attacks the false healers and they flee wounded and naked. Some of this passage is difficult to understand, but it speaks volumes about motive. And it is a good place to make application to life.

Application to Life

How important do you think it was for Paul to go back again and again to places he had been before to encourage those of The Way? What do you think he taught them? He taught about the kingdom of God. Why not read the Sermon on the Mount, Matthew 5 – 7. It is about the kingdom of God. Read Matthew 13 for some of Jesus' parables about the kingdom.

Motive is important for those of The Way, the followers of Jesus. Why do you do the good things you do? The magic workers wanted to make money from Jesus' power. Not a good reason to heal. Take time to discuss and think about your motives. Sometimes it is difficult to see our own selfishness. Discuss the idea that much of the healing ministry today may be motivated by corporate greed.

Prayer: *Dear Jesus, help us walk in your Way, motivated by love, Amen*

Paul and the Uproar in Ephesus
Acts 19:21-41

Introduction

This is a second study on Paul's stay of about three years in Ephesus. In the previous study (Acts 18:23-19:20) Paul had met with opposition from some of the Jews in the synagogue and had moved his teaching to a public meeting place. There he had met opposition from some magicians who wanted to buy the power of the Holy Spirit so they could profit by his power. A possessed man had over powered them and sent them running, wounded and naked. Many became followers of the Way. In this lesson Paul unveiled his present and future mission plan and was protected from another uproar over his interference with an economic segment of the society. Read Acts 19:21-41 and look for those plans and the uproar in Ephesus. Look for names of those who have joined in Paul's missionary efforts.

Paul Revealed His Mission Travel Plan

Did you see Paul's plan? He is intending to go see the churches in Macedonia, deliver their gifts to the poor saints in Jerusalem and then go to Rome. So much said in very few words in Acts 19:21-22.

Which churches in Macedonia and Achaia: Thessalonica, Berea, Philippi, and Corinth? His trip has the purpose of encouraging them. But on this trip Paul was collecting offerings for the poor saints in Jerusalem. You may recall a subtitle to the previous study. It said Paul wrote I Corinthians (a letter) to the church in Corinth while in Ephesus. In chapter 16, verses 1-3 he wrote: "Now about the collection for God's people. Do what I told the Galatians churches to do. On the first day of every week, each one of you should set aside a sum of money in keeping with his income, saving it up, so that when I come no collection will have to be made." Then he told them that they could choose men to accompany the gift to Jerusalem.

There were at least two reasons for this offering. One, of course, there was a concern for the poor. That always ought to be a concern of Christians, as it is for Jesus. No doubt all these towns had poor with needs. Why take an offering to Jerusalem? That is the second reason: to enlist the peace and unity of the church in Jerusalem. If Gentile Christians sent an offering to poor Jewish Christians, maybe those Jewish Christians in Jerusalem, who thought Gentiles must be converted to Judaism in order to follow Christ, would change their minds. Actions do speak louder than words.

Paul Was Protected from the Uproar in Ephesus

As in other places, Paul had preached that there is only one God. Idols were not to be worshipped. In Ephesus there was a huge following of a goddess named Artemis. She was a goddess of fertility. She is depicted as a woman with many breasts. There was a large temple in Ephesus dedicated to her worship. Replicas of her, made of silver, were sold. Demetrius, a silversmith, was losing money because people were turning from the worship of Artemis to the true God, made known in Jesus.

The silversmiths caused an uproar. They brought two of Paul's companions into the theater. Paul wanted to go with them because he was the one blamed. But his friends would not allow Paul to enter. A wise town ruler recognized the matter was about money and ordered the accusers to settle their dispute outside court. He feared that the uproar would get the attention of the Roman authorities and the whole town would suffer for what the silversmiths were causing. Paul saw that this was a good time to depart.

Application to Life

Count the ways Paul did his work in partnership. How do you and your group share partnership in your ministry? Read II Corinthians 9 for direction in giving. Discuss how to relate to those who believe differently from you.

Prayer: *Lord, teach us to be respectful and generous to those who differ with us. Amen*

Paul in Greece and Troas
Acts 20:1-12

Introduction

Sometimes the spiritual can be extremely practical. So, it is with this study. Please read the scripture text, Acts 20:1-12, now. This lesson will deal primarily with Paul's purpose of the third journey. There are at least four objectives that Paul had in mind: to gain more followers of Jesus; to encourage those who were already followers; to gather an offering for the poor in Jerusalem; and to insure the integrity of the offering's delivery. There is an incident in the study that may make your wince and smile at the same time. It, also, has some practical lessons.

Practical Purposes of Paul's Missionary Journey

The first two purposes have been discussed in previous studies. Only a few words of reminder will be given here. The purpose of all the journeys was to share the good news that Jesus was the Jewish Messiah or Christ. But not just for Jews; he was the Christ for the whole world. Jesus mission was to let the whole world know that God loves all people, in fact, his whole creation.

To the credit of Paul's wisdom, he returned again and again to the groups of Jesus followers to encourage them. They faced persecution in many places and ways, as did Paul. That was a major purpose of the letters he wrote to churches and individuals. Look at the letters ascribed to Paul. Romans through Titus in the New Testament are attributed to Paul. Many scholars believe the genuine Paul letters are: Romans, I

& II Corinthians, Galatians, Philippians, Colossians, Philemon, and I Thessalonians.

There were many poor Jewish followers of Jesus in Jerusalem. Acts 2:44-45 hints of this: "All the believers were together and had everything in common. Selling their possessions and goods, they gave to anyone as he had need." Some of the needs may have been temporary, others would have been ongoing.

Not only did Paul get the churches to give, but he suggested, maybe insisted, that they send persons from each church to accompany the offering. Why do you think he would do this? Here are a couple of suggestions. One would be to insure the integrity and safety of the offering. Paul may not have wanted the responsibility. He knew that the givers would like their offering to be delivered in tact by trustworthy persons from their own group.

Second, it was in the practical wisdom of Paul to have Greek believers to take the offering to the Jewish recipients. Something about meeting people face to face breaks down barriers of prejudice and suspicion. The believers would be able to see that their benefactors were people like themselves. This is practical wisdom.

In an earlier study it was suggested that you keep a list of Paul's new friends and helpers. Reread 20:4-6 for a list of those who would accompany him and the gifts to Jerusalem. Did you notice the "us" and "we" in verses 5 and 6? That means that the writer of Acts, Luke, has rejoined the traveling party. Though Paul is the main character in this study, he had a lot of help from other men and women.

Paul and a Young Man Named Eutychus

The story in verses 7 – 12 is interesting and may be humorous. Paul is in Troas, on his way to Jerusalem. He knows he may never see these folks again. He has a lot to say to them and they probably have a lot of questions for Paul. His discussion with them lasts into the night. They are in an upstairs room. A young man named Eutychus was seated by a window. He went to sleep and fell out of the window. They rushed down stairs. Paul threw himself on the young man and said that he is alive.

This story is the source of a lot of jokes about long sermons. But have you ever taken night classes as an adult? You get up early morning, work all day, go to a night class. If you never went to sleep in class, you have felt like it. Paul continues the discussion till morning and departs.

Application to Life

There is the matter of giving, read II Corinthians 9. Think about modern day wisdom concerning giving. There are hundreds of "Christian" and other organizations that are helping people in need. To whom should you give?

Check the financial reports of you church or other organizations to which you decide to give. How is the money being spent? How much is used to help people in your community? How much goes to other mission causes? How much goes to salaries? How much is spent on buildings? Learn what is being done, and by whom, in your community to: feed and clothe the poor; provide reasonable cost housing; meet medical and health needs; provide jobs, job training, transportation and money management.

Think about and discuss how you are dependent on others as you do mission work. The work requires cooperation, participation, coordination, and sharing.

Prayer: *Give us wisdom Lord, in our giving and service. Amen*

Paul Sailed to Caesarea
Acts 21:1-14

Introduction

In this study Luke, the author of Acts, continues his travel log of Paul's journey to Jerusalem. This is the end of his third missionary journey. He had as his travel companions his regular team members such as Luke. But Paul had insisted that at least one person from each of the churches that have made a contribution go along to deliver the offering. Recall, if you have done the previous study, Paul had collected an offering from the churches for the poor in Jerusalem. As noted earlier, there are at least two reasons for the offering. One is obvious and Jesus like: feed the poor. There was also the motive that the gentile givers might be accepted by the Jewish Christians in Jerusalem. A major problem in that time was that some Jewish believers in Jesus felt that gentiles had to accept certain Jewish practices, such as circumcision, in order to be accepted by Jesus. Paul strongly disagreed with that.

Stop here and read the text for this study; Acts 21:1-14. Note that Luke gave some detail about three stops on this part of the Journey. They spend seven days in Tyre; one day in Ptolemais; and in Caesarea "a number of days."

Paul Spent Seven Days in Tyre

Paul and his party were passengers on a merchant ship. When it docked to unload in Tyre, they disembarked and found a group of Jesus people and spent seven days with them. They reported that the Spirit was warning then that Paul should not go to Jerusalem. Trouble was waiting for his there. But Paul was insistent that he must continue his journey. The disciples followed Paul and his companions to the beach. There they held a prayer meeting for God's will to be done. They gave a tearful farewell as Paul's group boarded a ship to sail south.

Paul Spent One Day in Ptolemais

Luke does not tell us what happened during the visit with disciples at Ptolemais. He does tell us that they were there for one day. Can we assume that they also prayed with him? Do you think that they also may have urged him not to go to Jerusalem? Do you find it interesting that there are believers in Jesus in all these cities along the way? Don't forget that Luke is only telling us about Paul's journeys. There must have been many missionary trips by other disciples of Jesus to many other cities and countries.

Paul Spent Several Days in Caesarea

Caesarea was the center of Roman power in that area. It was also a large port city. Paul will return there as a prisoner in a future study. Philip, the evangelist lived there. To learn of this Philip, read Acts chapters six and eight. In chapter six he was elected to distribute food to gentile widows. In chapter eight he preached in Samaria, Gaza and Caesarea. Luke gives wonderful stories about him. You may want to stop now and read them.

Do you find it interesting that Philip had seven unmarried daughters who were prophets? Keep this in mind for your later thinking and group discussion. What should women be permitted to do in church?

Agabus, like an Old Testament prophet, dramatized what Paul could expect in Jerusalem. He took Paul's belt or sash and bound his own hands and feet. He told them that he was demonstrating what would happen to the man the sash belonged to if he went to Jerusalem. Luke said he and the rest of the group joined in pleading with Paul not to go. But Paul was determined to go. Luke said; "we gave up and said, 'The Lord's will be done.'"

Application to Life

Give some thought to and discuss how Paul and his company found followers of Jesus in each city they came to. Use your computer or local library to research early church or Christian history. What place do you think women should have in church in the society in which you live? In the early church they spoke, taught, were deacons. Why not now?

How do you reconcile Paul's determination to go to Jerusalem when other believers said that the Spirit was saying he should not go? How do you know the will of God in your life: prayer, reading scripture, listening to friends, reading Christian writers, and circumstances?

Prayer: *God, give us wisdom to know and the courage to do your will. Amen*

Paul Met with the Ephesian Elders at Miletus
Acts 20:13-38

Introduction

The first part of this study reads like a travel log. It might be helpful to refer to a Bible map that shows the places mentioned. Paul and his friends from several churches are on their way to Jerusalem to deliver a gift of money for the poor. Paul makes part of the journey by land and alone. This may be because in the first part of chapter 20, he had planned to sail, but had learned of a plot to kill him. Read Acts 20:13-38 and note that the major teaching here has to do with what Paul thinks is his farewell address to the elders from the church at Ephesus. Paul plans to get to Jerusalem by Pentecost and does not want to be delayed. Therefore, he asks the elders to meet him at Miletus, on the coast, about 30 miles from Ephesus. In his address note how he: reminded them of his ministry with them; instructed the elders; and spoke of his commitment to continue his journey.

It would help you grasp the importance of this farewell address if you would take time now to read those of: Jacob in Genesis 49:1-17; Moses in Deuteronomy 33:1-29; Joshua in Joshua 23-24; David in I Kings 2:1-4 and Jesus in John 14-17.

Paul Reminded the Ephesians of His Ministry with Them

Paul seemed very proud and grateful for his vocation as a tentmaker or leather worker. By working with his hands as a livelihood he was not a financial burden to the church. His preaching and ministry were free. He also reminded them of his faithfulness in preaching and teaching the truth of Jesus to them. Remember that Paul's message, the good news, was Jesus is the Christ, the Messiah sent by God, He was sent to the Jews, but also to the whole world. They knew that Paul had spent a lot of time with them. They also knew that Paul had suffered a lot of persecution in order to stay with them.

Paul Told the Elders What They Were to Do

Paul uses a well-known Jewish metaphor to teach them. They are to shepherd their sheep. Shepherding goes all the way back to Abraham in the Old Testament (Hebrew Bible) stories. The metaphor is exemplified in the story of Moses leading the Hebrews through the desert. David was a shepherd. Read his poem about God being a shepherd in Psalm 23. Read Jeremiah 23 and Ezekiel 34 to see how the metaphor was used by the prophets. In John 10 Jesus said, "I am the good shepherd." Then Paul gave the elders warning that their job was not going to be easy. False teachers and others would oppose them. He encouraged to remain faithful.

Paul Committed Himself to Continue His Journey

"And now, compelled by the Spirit, I am going to Jerusalem, not knowing what will happen to me there. I only know that in every city the Holy Spirit warns me that prison and hardships are facing me. However, I consider my life worth nothing to me, if only I may finish the race and complete the task the Lord Jesus has given me – the task of testifying to the gospel of God's grace" Acts 20:22-24. That speaks for itself. What determination, dedication!

The next few studies will reveal what did happen. Paul was in prison in Rome at the end of Acts. But church history and tradition say that Paul was released and returned to Ephesus for a time before being imprisoned again and put to death.

Application to Life

Paul desired to get to Jerusalem by Pentecost, a Jewish harvest festival. Many people from near and far would be there. Why do you think Paul chose that time? Think, discuss, and write a list of shepherd duties. Using them as metaphors of what you should do to be a shepherd to others?

Give thought to your faithfulness in difficult times. List the things that help you to remain faithful when you are treated wrongly because of your faith.

Have you decided to place your faith in Jesus as Christ and follow him?

If not, will you do that now?

Prayer: *Lord, help us to be good shepherds to each other, as you are to us. Amen.*

Paul Sailed to Caesarea
Acts 21:1-14

Introduction

In this study Luke, the author of Acts, continues his travel log of Paul's journey to Jerusalem. This is the end of his third missionary journey. He had as his travel companions his regular team members such as Luke. But Paul had insisted that at least one person from each of the churches that have contributed go along to deliver the offering. Recall, if you have done the previous study, Paul had collected an offering from the churches for the poor in Jerusalem. As noted earlier, there are at least two reasons for the offering. One is obvious and Jesus like: feed the poor. There was also the motive that the gentile givers might be accepted by the Jewish Christians in Jerusalem. A major problem in that time was that some Jewish believers in Jesus felt that gentiles had to accept certain Jewish practices, such as circumcision, in order to be accepted by Jesus. Paul strongly disagreed with that.

Stop here and read the text for this study; Acts 21:1-14. Note that Luke gave some detail about three stops on this part of the Journey. They spend seven days in Tyre; one day in Ptolemais; and in Caesarea "a number of days."

Paul Spent Seven Days in Tyre

Paul and his party were passengers on a merchant ship. When it docked to unload in Tyre, they disembarked and found a group of Jesus people and spent seven days with them. They reported that the Spirit was warning then that Paul should not go to Jerusalem. Trouble was waiting for his there. But Paul was insistent that he must continue his journey. The disciples followed Paul and his companions to the beach. There they held a prayer meeting for God's will to be done. They gave a tearful farewell as Paul's group boarded a ship to sail south.

Paul Spent One Day in Ptolemais

Luke does not tell us what happened during the visit with disciples at Ptolemais. He does tell us that they were there for one day. Can we assume that they also prayed with him? Do you think that they also may have urged him not to go to Jerusalem? Do you find it interesting that there are believers in Jesus in all these cities along the way? Don't forget that Luke is only telling us about Paul's journeys. There must have been many missionary trips by other disciples of Jesus to many other cities and countries.

Paul Spent Several Days in Caesarea

Caesarea was the center of Roman power in that area. It was also a large port city. Paul will return there as a prisoner in a future study. Philip, the evangelist lived there. To learn of this Philip, read Acts chapters six and eight. In chapter six he was elected to distribute food to gentile widows. In chapter eight he preached in Samaria, Gaza and Caesarea. Luke gives wonderful stories about him. You may want to stop now and read them.

Do you find it interesting that Philip had seven unmarried daughters who were prophets? Keep this in mind for your later thinking and group discussion. What should women be permitted to do in church?

Agabus, like an Old Testament prophet, dramatized what Paul could expect in Jerusalem. He took Paul's belt or sash and bound his own hands and feet. He told them that he was demonstrating what would happen to the man the sash belonged to if he went to Jerusalem. Luke said he and the rest of the group joined in pleading with Paul not to go. But Paul was determined to go. Luke said; "we gave up and said, 'The Lord's will be done.'"

Application to Life

Give some thought to and discuss how Paul and his company found followers of Jesus in each city they came to. Use your computer or local library to research early church or Christian history.

What place do you think women should have in church in the society in which you live? In the early church they spoke, taught, were deacons. Why not now?

How do you reconcile Paul's determination to go to Jerusalem when other believers said that the Spirit was saying he should not go? How do you know the will of God in your life: prayer, reading scripture, listening to friends, reading Christian writers, and circumstances?

Prayer: *God, give us wisdom to know and the courage to do your will. Amen.*

Paul Met with the Jerusalem Church
Acts 21:15-26

Introduction

Against the better judgment of many, Paul continued his journey to Jerusalem. His traveling companions remained faithful and went with him. Some of the disciples in Caesarea joined Paul's group. They must have known a disciple in Jerusalem named Mnason. Mnason was a disciple from Cyprus. Do you recall anyone from Cyprus? What about Barnabas (Acts 4:36)? Also, recall Paul's first missionary journey (Acts 13:1-5).

Mnason invited the group to stay in his home. Do you guess that he may have been wealthy to have a house to hold Paul's group? Was it an act of courage to house the group, if he also knew that Paul's life was in danger?

Stop here and read the test for this study (Acts 21:15-26). Look for: Paul reported on his journey to James and the elders; Paul was faced with a challenge; and Paul accepted the challenge.

Paul Reported to James and the Elders

Paul and his companions went to see James, who seemed to be the leader of the disciples of Jesus in Jerusalem. The elders, assumed leaders, also met with them. Paul related all the things the God had been doing with the Gentiles on his journey. You think he may have presented the offering from the gentile believers at this time? James and the elders praised God for what they heard.

Then James related to Paul and his companions that there were thousands of Jewish followers of Jesus who felt strongly that gentile believers must follow Jewish traditions and law observances. So, Paul's report sounded wonderful, BUT!

Paul is Presented a Challenge

James wanted Paul to show his faithfulness to the Jewish believers by supporting a Jewish rite of vows. Four men have made a vow. There was a cost involved, so Paul is asked not only to go to the temple with the vow makers, but also pay their expense. Some think this was asking Paul to compromise. Think about that. Was it not a natural thing for Paul to do this? Or was he going against a conviction that he no longer needed to do this type of religious ritual? The question arises, when did the church separate from the temple? When did Christianity become distinct from Judaism? There is one and the same God in Old Testament and New Testament.

Paul Accepted the Challenge

Verse 26 tells us the story: "The next day Paul took the men and purified himself along with them. Then he went to the temple to give notice of the date when the days of purification would end, and the offering would be made for each of them." The vow included shaving the head, probably another expense that Paul agreed to pay. Had Paul made a similar vow himself (Acts 18:18)? A lot is not known about what took place. The point is that Paul was willing to participate in this Jewish ritual. The question is: was he compromising his loyalty to Jesus in doing so? Or did Paul have no problem with doing what he had done before as a loyal Jew? Was Paul expressing an inclusive faith as opposed to exclusive? In the following lessons it will be made clear that Paul's enemies were not so generous as Paul. They are after him and will do whatever it takes to be rid of him. Remind you of Jesus' experience?

Application to Life

How important is it to respect the religious beliefs and practices of others? How important is it to stay connected with the church and church leaders as Paul did? Do you think that Paul still considered himself a good Jew as far as religion was concerned? Remember his message was that Jesus was/is the Jewish Messiah. But Paul saw him as the Messiah of the world.

Prayer: *Lord, thank you for our heritage, we believe Jesus is Lord of all. Amen*

Paul Arrested in Jerusalem
Acts 21:27-40; 22:1-29

Introduction

This study is of mob psychology and violence. This is not unlike mob activity today. It seems to happen regardless of race, religion, place or issue. Read the text, Acts 21:27-40 and 22:1-19. Note how Paul was falsely accused using generalizations and assumptions. The civil authority calmed the violence and rescued Paul to protect itself.

Paul made his defense but had to remain under civil protection from the religious radicals. Watch for commonalities of what happened to Paul and radical demonstrations and violence in your community or country.

Paul was Accused of Religious Violations

Some Jews from Asia were in Jerusalem and learned that Paul was there in the temple. They incited a riot. They dragged Paul from the temple and shouted to the crowd that Paul was against: their people, the Jews; the law; and this place, the temple. These are all generalizations. It is foddering to feed unthinking people who are looking for something to be against. The other accusation was an assumption, not fact. Someone had seen Paul in Jerusalem with Trophimus, a Greek. They ASSUMED that Paul had taken him into the temple. So, what, there was a place in the temple for gentiles. The insinuation, another mob technique, was that he had taken him into the place for Jewish men. That place was forbidden to gentiles.

The crowd was agitated enough to attack Paul and would probably have killed him had he not been rescued.

Paul Was Rescued by Civil Authorities

The crowd raised enough noise and disruption that the Roman military or police authority was sent to quell the riot. They rescued Paul and arrested him on ASSUMPTION that he was an Egyptian who had caused an earlier riot. Of course, a major reason for Paul being rescued and arrested was to stop the riot. The military were there to make sure peace was secured. Their jobs and perhaps lives were at stake. Rome permitted no uprisings by the people. As the soldiers were about to bodily carry Paul into their "fort," Paul spoke to the leader in Greek. Surprised, the soldier asked how he, an assumed Egyptian, can speak Greek. That gave Paul an opportunity to tell who he was and give his testimony to the crowd. Reread this now in Acts 21:37- 22:21. You also can read Paul's conversion experience in Acts chapter nine.

The crowd listened till he said God sent him to the gentiles. Then they resumed their cries for his death. So, he was taken inside and was about to be beaten and questioned to find the truth. Paul at that point told them they were about to beat a Roman citizen. That would certainly bring trouble for them. The commander was told, and he went to talk with Paul. It would be good for you to reread Acts 22:25-29. There is interesting information about Roman citizenship. Paul claimed Roman citizenship by birth, the commander said he had to buy his citizenship.

It appears Paul was then kept overnight for his safety and so Paul could be questioned by the Jewish religious high court, called the Sanhedrin. That will be the next study. Application to Life

Think about and discuss with your group: how important is it for you to think for yourself? How often do you make decisions about others based on assumptions? How often do you use generalizations to classify people? Do you ever say "All (fill in the blank) persons are bad, evil, ignorant, (you fill in the word)? Do you use this kind of thinking about other races, religions, (you name the group)?

Discuss with your group the importance of separation of church and state. It is dangerous when either controls the other. Both Jesus and Paul experienced the religious group appeal to Rome to do their dirty work.

Prayer: *Lord, help us to think for ourselves and not assume or generalize. Amen.*

Paul Before Felix
Acts 24:1-27

Introduction

In the last study Paul had been arrested in Jerusalem and faced trial by the Sanhedrin, the high court of the Jews. When Paul spoke of resurrection from the dead the court became an argument between the Sadducees, who did not believe in resurrection, and the Pharisees, who did believe in resurrection. The argument became so violent that the Roman authority feared for Paul's safety and stopped the proceedings. A plot to have Paul killed was discovered and the Roman authority had Paul transferred to the Judean capitol, Caesarea. This study is about what took place five days later in Caesarea. Paul was accused; he denied the accusations; decision was made to continue to hold him.

Paul Before Governor Felix

Five days after Paul was taken to Caesarea, the high priest, Ananias, along with some elders and a lawyer named Tertullus came from Jerusalem to make their case against Paul before Felix, the governor.

Tertullus opening speech sounds very much like a politician of today. He praised the governor and then launched in to tell him what he wanted him to believe. In fact, he attempted to put his words in the mouth of Felix. The charges against Paul were much the same as the trial in Jerusalem.

Paul had disturbed Jews everywhere ("all over the world"). He was ring leader of the Nazarenes. This was a term used to describe Jesus' followers. Probably this was a sarcastic term denoting Jesus being from Nazareth in Galilee. The third charge was that Paul had desecrated the temple. That is probably a reference to the assumption in the last study, that Paul had taken a gentile into the temple. Verse nine indicates that the others in the prosecuting party from Jerusalem gave their agreement to Tertullus' charges.

Paul Defended Himself

Paul denied the charges. But he said, concerning being a follower of the Way, he worshipped the God of the Jews in that Way. Jesus was the Jewish Messiah. Paul took this opportunity to testify to a clear conscience. He also told about coming to Jerusalem to bring the offering for the poor in Jerusalem.

A third part of his defense is that the ones who began this trouble were not present. He reminded them, it was some Jews from Asia who had brought the charges against him and they were not there to face him.

Felix Adjourned the Court

Verse 22, "Then Felix, who was well acquainted with the Way, adjourned the proceedings." He indicated that a decision would be made later. Felix seemed to have a real interest in Paul and the Way. He gave instruction to the centurion to keep Paul under guard but give him some freedom and to allow his friends to visit and take care of his needs.

Felix brought his wife, a Jewess, to listen to Paul. It appears that Felix was very near becoming a follower of Jesus. After two years Felix was succeeded as governor by Festus. Paul will have opportunity to testify before Festus and his wife also, Acts 25 and 26.

Application to Life

Paul seemed to find more understanding and civil treatment by the Roman authorities than the religious leaders. Think about what you know of religious history and note how off the path of love and compassion it can get. The Way of the followers of Jesus should be the best at loving and caring for others. They should be compassionate and loving toward all, regard less of race and religion. Christianity should seek the "common good" for all. Discuss this with your study group.

Prayer: *Lord, help us to be compassionate and loving toward all people. Amen.*

Paul Before the Sanhedrin and Escorted to Caesarea
Acts 22:30 23:1-35

Introduction

In the last two studies Paul and his companions had come to Jerusalem to bring an offering from the churches he had visited on his third missionary journey. The offering was for the poor in Jerusalem. He met with James and the church leaders. Then he met with opposition by some Jews from Asia and a mob incited by them. The Roman soldiers rescued him and held him overnight. The following day Paul was presented to the highest Jewish court, called the Sanhedrin. That is where this study begins. At this point read how Paul expressed his innocence and was confronted by the high priest. Then Paul used a "divide and conquer" technique to prove his innocence. A plan to assassinate him caused him to be transferred to Caesarea.

Paul Was Tried Before the Sanhedrin

The Roman official called for a meeting of the Jewish high court, called the Sanhedrin. He knew that whatever Paul was being accused of had nothing to do with Roman civil law. Paul proclaimed his innocence and the high priest had him struck in the face. Paul retaliated with very strong words, some would say a type of curse. Paul was condemned for saying such to a high priest. Paul denied knowing that Ananias was the high priest. Some think that this was a sarcastic reply; that Paul did know who he was but was unworthy to be high priest. The trial continued.

Paul Used a Divide and Conquer Technique

Paul denied their generalized charge, that he stirred up all the Jews. But he confessed to being a strict follower of the Way. In fact, he worshipped the God of the Jews through this Way, that is by being a follower of Jesus. He realized his accusers were made up of both Pharisees and Sadducees. So, Paul told of Jesus' resurrection. The Sadducees did not believe in resurrection, but the Pharisees did. This began an argument between the two groups. It became so conflictive that the Roman officer stopped the trial and took Paul back to the Roman fort for safety. Paul Was Transferred to Caesarea

A group of forty men made a covenant that they would not eat till they had killed Paul. Paul's sister's son heard about this and got word to the Roman official. The official believed the plot to be true. He made plans and had Paul escorted by a host of soldiers to Caesarea. The journey began that night. When they came to gentile territory many of the soldiers returned to Jerusalem. The others continued to escort Paul to the Judean capitol in Caesarea. The next two studies will tell of the trials and events there. His imprisonment there lasted for two years. Do you suppose the men with the vow changed their minds and ate?

Application to Life

Give thought to how strict beliefs can trap you into being so dogmatic that you cannot accept change in belief or respect those with differing beliefs. Where do your beliefs come from? Examine these possibilities. How were your beliefs shaped in early childhood by your environment and culture? What did your parents believe? What about the holy writings used in your culture and by your parents? How did your church, synagogue, mosque or other holy place shape your beliefs? What about your experiences of the holy or God? Note how Paul three times in the book of Acts tells of the experience he had on the road from Jerusalem to Damascus. The experience is recorded in Acts 9.

Do you see Paul in this study faced with the choice of respecting, (he did respect), the Jewish synagogue, scripture and practices? He experienced Jesus as the Jewish Messiah, Paul knew him to be the Messiah of the whole world. Discuss ways you can meet and share with those who differ from you. How can you listen to their story and tell them yours?

Prayer: *Lord, may we be faithful in sharing our experience of you with others. Amen*

Paul Before Festus and Agrippa
Acts 25:1-27; 26:1-32

Introduction

As you see, the text for this study is long, chapters 25 and 26 of Acts. Read them now. Paul had already had a couple of "trials" in Jerusalem, religious and civil. Paul had been sent to Caesarea, the Roman capitol of the province, because of a plot to assassinate him. His accusers had come soon afterward, and Paul was tried before Felix the governor, who delayed the process because he found nothing criminal against Paul.

Paul's Trials Continued

For some time, Paul was still being held in Caesarea, Felix was replaced by Festus as governor. While on a week to ten-day visit in Jerusalem, Festus is requested by Paul's enemies to have Paul brought back to Jerusalem for trial. Not wanting to delay his trip back home to Caesarea, Festus tells them to come to Caesarea to present their charges against Paul.

The Jerusalem enemy came down, Festus convened the court, and Paul again stated his innocence. The enemy again asked that Paul be brought back to Jerusalem for trial. Festus. desired to do them a favor, so he faced Paul with going back to Jerusalem. Paul proclaimed that his Roman trial is in the right place, that is Caesarea. Rather than go back to Jerusalem, he appealed to Caesar. That is, as a Roman citizen he claimed his right to be tried in Rome, Festus accepted his appeal. Paul then began a long wait, nearly two years, before he was sent to Rome.

Paul Made the Most of His Opportunities

Strange and sometimes wonderful things can take place in spite of undesired circumstances. Did you see that taking place with Paul as you read the text? He was in prison but was given some freedom for movement and for having visitors. Don't you imagine that Paul used these opportunities to preach and to teach? Do you think that he might have written letters to friends and churches to instruct and encourage them?

From the text it seems that Festus heard Paul on other occasions. In addition, Roman puppet King Agrippa met Paul. He was king of Galilee and Peraea. He and his wife Bernice had come for an extended visit with Festus on the coast. Bernice was also his sister and the sister of Felix's wife, Drusilla.

Festus told Agrippa about Paul. Agrippa expressed an interest in meeting Paul. Therefore, Festus arranged a royal sort of court hearing with Agrippa and Bernice decked out in royal finery. Paul was brought before them to testify. Paul appealed to Agrippa's knowledge of Hebrew scripture and justice. Did you note that this was at least three times you have read Paul's conversion experience? He also appealed to his own faithfulness to the vision and obedience to the voice of Jesus. Luke told the feelings of the audience. "The king rose, and with him the governor and Bernice and those sitting with them. They left the room and while talking with one another, they said, 'This man is not doing anything that deserves death or imprisonment.' Agrippa said to Festus, 'This man could have been set free if he had not appealed to Caesar,' Acts 26:30-32.

Is this not a good example of giving testimony of personal experience and leaving the results to the Spirit of God? The story does not tell us what changes may have taken place in the lives of those who heard. The next study, Acts 27, is a great story of sea travel and ship wreck. As you read it look again for how God works in strange circumstance and wonderful ways to accomplish his will.

Application to Life

Think of times in your life when troubles seemed to continue to pile up and not go away. Can you look back and see how God may have been working in and through bad circumstances to bring about good? Have you had opportunity to proclaim your faith to others during a difficult time? Recall that it was Paul's desire to go to Rome. Do you think he felt that going as a prisoner was a surprising way for his desire to be realized?

Prayer: *Lord, may we be faithful and see you in all circumstances of life. Amen*

Paul's Voyage and Shipwreck
Acts 27:1-44

Introduction

This study has to do with sea travel and shipwreck. Luke gives a detailed account of Paul's journey from Caesarea, where he had spent two years as a prisoner, to Rome. Most of the journey was by sea. Luke indicates that he is with Paul. Aristarchus from Thessalonica was with them. From previous studies you may remember that when Paul came to Jerusalem, he brought a gift from the churches for the poor in Jerusalem. Each church had sent one or more persons to accompany Paul and the gifts. Do you think some of these were on this trip to Rome? A Roman centurion (soldier in charge of one hundred) went to escort Paul. Luke does not tell how many other soldiers went with the centurion.

Stop here and read Acts chapter 27. It is one of the longer chapters in Acts. That may indicate Luke's love for travel. It would be a great help to use a map to follow the trip. Two other stormy sea trips may be interesting to read along with this one: The short book of Jonah and another by Luke in the Gospel of Luke chapter 8:22-25. Read Psalm 107:23-31 for a graphic description of danger in a storm on the sea. This study will deal with the trip from the time Paul warns the captain of the ship and the owner that it was a dangerous thing to set out from where they were. Note how Paul placed his confidence in his vision and how he took charge in the dangerous storm.

Paul Warned of Danger

The ship owner and the captain knew that time for winter sailing was not good. They decided to move to Phoenix, another port in the southwest of Crete. Paul warned them that it was a bad idea. They rejected his advice. Do you think you might have done the same if you were a sea captain and a prisoner, who was some kind of preacher, advised you? Any way, they set sail only to be driven out to sea by a strong wind called a "northeaster." This was the beginning of their troubles which lasted for at least two weeks (verse 21). But does verse 14 indicate that they had already been at sea days before the 14 referred to in 27:21?

Paul Had a Vision and Took Charge

At some point in all the turmoil Paul had a vision. An angel told him that he must stand before Caesar and that no one on the ship would lose their life. Reread verse 23. The story from there on shows Paul in charge. He acted and spoke with such authority that the captain and the centurion accepted his word. On two occasions the text says Paul ate and encouraged them to eat. They would need nourishment to endure the work and effort to be saved. He blessed, broke and ate bread before them. He did what he asked them to do. The scene is almost Jesus like, in giving thanks, breaking and eating together

As the sailors determined that they were near an island, they attempt to desert the ship. Paul again took charge. He told the centurion, "Unless these men stay with the ship, you cannot be saved" verse 31. So, the soldiers cut the ropes to the life boat on which the sailors planned to escape.

Paul directed the escape operation for them all when the ship got stuck on a sand bar and was destroyed. All made it safe to a strange island on which strange things would transpire. But that is for the next study, Acts 28:1-16.

Application to Life

Recall a time when you were afraid. Did you in any way think that God was right there with you in your scary time? What do you think of Paul's advice to take care of the physical (he told them to eat) in time of trouble and distress? Did you know that one of the most often used phrases attributed to God or Jesus in the Bible is: "Do not be afraid" or "Fear not?"

Do you find it difficult to speak out when you disagree on something important? Think of times when racial or religious slurs are spoken.

Is that a time to kindly take a stand for the image of God in all persons?

Should this affect the way you vote and the way you live simply and honestly?

Do you believe with confidence that God's Spirit is at work in your life and circumstances even when things are not good? Remember Paul was a prisoner and enduring a life-threatening storm.

Prayer: *God, thank you for being with us at all times, even in the storms. Amen*

Paul on Malta and on to Rome
Acts 28:1-10

Introduction

The previous study concluded with Paul shipwrecked on an unknown island. He was being transported as a prisoner to Rome. He had at least two traveling companions in addition to a centurion and soldiers sent to guard him. There was also the ship's crew. The total was 276 according to most scripture versions. This study deals with what took place on the island. Read the study test in Acts 28:1-10.

Consider the attitude and actions of the native people, the "main" citizen of the island, and Paul. The People of Malta Were Hospitable Upon their arrival on the island the shipwrecked survivors discovered the island was Malta. It is about fifty miles south of Rome. Today Malta has a population of nearly one half million. It is strongly Roman Catholic. As on the sea, it was cold and raining on Malta. "The islanders showed us unusual kindness. They built a fire and welcomed us all because it was raining and cold," verse 2. Hospitality and kindness are Jesus like actions.

Paul helped gather wood for the fire. But there was a snake in the sticks he picked up and it bit his hand and held on. Paul shook it off into the fire. The islanders had some feeling or sense of justice. They were sure Paul must have been a murderer or bad criminal because the snake, they thought to be poisonous, bit him. They expected him to die. When he did not, they changed their minds and thought Paul was a god. Were they superstitious? Probably, but does it not speak well of them that they could and did "change their minds?" Publius Was the Chief Official

Again, note the hospitality. The "regular" islanders showed kindness. So, did the leading citizen. "He welcomed us to his home and for three days entertained us hospitably," verse 7. Do you think he was influenced by what he may have heard from the "islanders?" Actions speak loudly, do they not? Verse 10 may apply to the first "islanders" who welcomed the shipwrecked, or it could apply to Publius, or to those who were healed and their kin. The verse says, "They honored us in many ways and when we were ready to sail, they furnished us with the supplies we needed." Do you think "they" means all the above?

Paul Responded with Truth and Healing

Luke does not give Paul's response to the "islanders" thought; that he was a god. Don't you think Paul took that as an opportunity to deny that and tell them about the one God who loves all people? We are told that Publius" father was ill. Paul went to see him, prayed for him and put his hand on him. He was healed. The word quickly spread, and many brought their sick to be cured. Does it not appear that there was a lot of mutual sharing in this story? Though Luke does not tell us, it is assumed that Paul and his friends told these new friends about Jesus and his love for them. Do you think that these people had already heard about Jesus?

With provisions provided by these new friends, Paul and company continue their journey to Rome. That is our next and final study. Read it in Acts 28:11-31.

Application to Life

You surely have in your mind life lessons from this study. Add your list to the following few. One lesson is to be kind to strangers and people in need. It might be good to make a list: people from other lands or even nearby places; people who are sick and handicapped; people of other religions, backgrounds, economic standing. Consider how God opens doors for help and for witness in times of trouble. Are you open to changing your mind about people and beliefs? Is it possible that others may know aspects of truth that you do not know?

Prayer: *Lord, may we be open to truth and be kind to everyone. Amen*

Paul in Rome
Acts 28: 11-31

Introduction

The final verses of Acts tell of Paul's last fifty miles by sea and land to get to Rome. Read the text now, Acts 28:11-31. Note the help along the way, Paul preached in his own rented house and the unhindered gospel.

Paul Was Met by Encouragers

After three months Paul makes the final fifty-mile journey into Rome. After a portion of this journey is made by sea, Paul is met by fellow followers of Jesus. They come to greet and encourage him. Must have been extremely refreshing, don't you think?

Upon arriving in Rome Paul called for the Jewish leaders to explain the charges against him by some in Jerusalem. He also stated his innocence of the charges. They report that they know nothing about the charges and that those they have seen from Jerusalem in Rome did not mention them. This must have encouraged Paul.

Paul Preached in Rome

Paul was placed under guard in a house for which he paid the rent. He had freedom to have guests. Many came to hear him teach about the kingdom of God. He continued to proclaim that Jesus was the hoped-for Messiah. Many of the Jews believed his message about Jesus, but many did not believe.

The important matter here is that Paul's dream of preaching in Rome came true, but in a most unusual way. Did he ever go on to Spain, as was his desire?

Luke does not tell us. He does say that Paul spent two years in Rome.

Paul Wrote in Rome

Paul kept busy. We learn from some of his letters that they were written while he was in prison. Surely some of them were written during this time of being in prison in Rome. There are theories of Paul being in prison in Ephesus and then again in Rome. You may want to research that, the purpose here is to study what Luke tells in Acts. Read the following passages to get an idea of what and why Paul wrote in prison: Ephesians 6:19-20; Philippians 1:12-26; Colossians 4:2-18. II Timothy 4:9-18; and Philemon verse 23.

As you noted in each of these passages a great number of names were called. On the negative side, some had deserted Paul, and no one was present for a trial it seems. On the positive side, Paul had scads of friends who did remain faithful to Jesus, the Christ. Paul recognized his dependence on them for both encouragement and financial support.

As a closing example of Paul's witness and friendship; of his openness and persuasive power; and of his love for all and community, read his short letter to Philemon. It is a letter to a friend to be read before the church. It pleads with power for Philemon to accept a runaway slave back into his household, not as a slave, but as a brother. A great way to close a study of the unhindered Gospel.

Unhindered Gospel

Frank Stagg, a past generation New Testament scholar entitled his excellent book on the study of Acts "The Unhindered Gospel." Unhindered is the last word in Luke's writing of Acts.

And so, it is the unhindered and continuing gospel. It was no mistake that Luke ends Acts as he does. Do you think your life is writing one of those continuing chapters of the gospel? God did not end his work with creation nor with the life, death and resurrection of Jesus. He continues his work through the people and events of history. Every follower of Jesus is a participant. The question is, "What are you writing with your life?"

Application to Life

The obvious lesson for this closing study is that Paul let nothing hinder his passion for proclaiming the love of God for all people and creation as revealed in and through Jesus Christ. Through criticism, threats, storms, trials and jails, sickness and handicaps he remained faithful. Determine what you will study next. Consider "The Jesus Story: Musings for Meditation and Application."

Prayer: *Dear God, help us to be faithful to you throughout all of life. Amen*

www.ingramcontent.com/pod-product-compliance
Lightning Source LLC
Chambersburg PA
CBHW052201110526
44591CB00012B/2031